THE   MURMURING   GRIEF   OF   THE   AMERICAS

THE MURMURING GRIEF OF THE AMERICAS

THE MURMURING GRIEF OF
                  THE AMERICAS

THE   MURMURING   GRIEF   OF   THE   AMERICAS

THE MURMURING GRIEF

                OF THE AMERICAS OF THE AMERICAS THE MURMURING

GRIEF OF THE AMERICAS

THE MURMURING THE MURMURING THE MURMURING THE MURMURING
THE GRIEF THE GRIEF THE GRIEF THE GRIEF THE GRIEF THE GRIEF

THE   MURMURING   GRIEF   OF

                THE AMERICAS

MURMURMURMURMURMURMURMURMURMURMURMURMURMURMUR
MUR

EXCUSE ME, SIR, WHAT TIME IS THE MASSACRE?

THE MURMURING GRIEF OF THE AMERICAS   MURMUR MURMUR

MURMUR

THE   MURMURING   GRIEF   OF   THE   AMERICAS

THE MURMURING GRIEF OF THE AMERICAS

ALSO BY DANIEL BORZUTZKY,
FROM COFFEE HOUSE PRESS

Written After a Massacre in the Year 2018

THE MURMURING GRIEF
OF THE AMERICAS

Daniel Borzutzky

COFFEE HOUSE PRESS

Minneapolis

2024

The author photograph is by Patri Hadad and is courtesy of the University of Arizona Poetry Center, copyright © 2018 by the Arizona Board of Regents.

Coffee House Press books are available to the trade through our primary distributor, Consortium Book Sales & Distribution, cbsd.com or (800) 283-3572. For personal orders, catalogs, or other information, write to info@coffeehousepress.org.

Coffee House Press is a nonprofit literary publishing house. Support from private foundations, corporate giving programs, government programs, and generous individuals helps make the publication of our books possible. We gratefully acknowledge their support in detail in the back of this book.

LIBRARY OF CONGRESS CATALOGING-IN-PUBLICATION DATA

Names: Borzutzky, Daniel, author.
Title: Murmuring grief of the Americas / Daniel Borzutzky.
Other titles: Murmuring grief of the Americas (Compilation)
Description: Minneapolis : Coffee House Press, 2024.
Identifiers: LCCN 2024002592 (print) | LCCN 2024002593 (ebook) | ISBN 9781566897051 (paperback) | ISBN 9781566897068 (epub)
Subjects: LCGFT: Poetry.
Classification: LCC PS3602.O79 M87 2024 (print) | LCC PS3602.O79 (ebook) | DDC 811/.6—dc23/eng/20240212
LC record available at https://lccn.loc.gov/2024002592
LC ebook record available at https://lccn.loc.gov/2024002593

PRINTED IN THE UNITED STATES OF AMERICA

31 30 29 28 27 26 25 24   1 2 3 4 5 6 7 8

CONTENTS

Of Glory not a Beam is left
But her Eternal House –
The Asterisk is for the Dead,
The Living, for the Stars

Emily Dickinson

I shall miss myself so much when I die

Clarice Lispector

I shall miss myself so much when I die

Clarice Lispector

Of Glory not a Beam is left
But her Eternal House –
The Asterisk is for the Dead,
The Living, for the Stars

Emily Dickinson

I shall miss myself so much when I die

Clarice Lispector

I shall miss myself so much when I die

Clarice Lispector

Of Glory not a Beam is left
But her Eternal House –
The Asterisk is for the Dead,
The Living, for the Stars

Emily Dickinson

THE MURMURING GRIEF
OF THE AMERICAS

****** is for the dead ******* ******* is for the dead *******

The living for the ★ ★ ★ The living for the ★ ★ ★

The Murmuring Grief of the Americas

there are children crossing the river   some float on cardboard and some
hold on to each other and some sing *we are alive*   there are neon lights
above the river   the camera crews stand on the banks and film the river
in the right light   they film the floating children in the right light   they
film the sky turning purple and pink as fluffy pollen dissolves in the
warm air   a tree with edible fruit is in the background   droopy white
flowers with long petals hang down and by the tree a brother and sister
exhausted

don't die   the director says to the children   if you die we won't be able
to make this film and if we don't make this film there will be no evidence
that once you were alive and if there is no evidence that once you were
alive   then no one will know that we loved you

the children step out of the river and walk to a bridge where there is a
sign that says *Welcome to the Promised Land*   but the sign is not meant
for the children   it is meant for the patriots who are chasing the children
the patriots do not enter the scene to be documented   they are there
to hunt the children   they try to trap the children on the bridge but
they do not arrive in time   they meet the children on the other side of
the bridge   where the camera records one of them saying welcome to
the promised land you little warthogs and there is gun shot   and the
children run off in different directions   the camera doesn't know whom
to follow   one child is shot in the leg and the camera zooms in on his
blood as the patriots drag him away

the camera catches up with the children later that night when they set up
camp on a spinach farm   the director takes great pleasure in filming
the older children as they care for the young ones   they feed them and
bathe them and sing songs and play games like Simon Says and Simon
tells the children to stop speaking   he tells the children to stop breathing
to stop wanting   to stop thinking   to stop being themselves   he tells
the children to become someone else   to become something else   and
the children say how do we do that   and Simon says you listen to the
earth   at the right time it will tell you what to do   but he knows the
earth is a liar

After Simon puts the children to bed the camera lingers on his face as
he weeps   and he tells himself   stop speaking   and he tells himself
stop breathing   and he tells himself   stop eating   and he looks into the
camera and says the pain in my mouth won't stop   this pain in my eyes
won't stop   my tongue is burning   my lips are burning   my soul needs
to rest he says   your soul?   stop breathing   he tells himself   I need
to die again he says   because when I die again I will become the river
that runs between myself and myself   I will become the mountains that
separate myself from myself   and you will deposit new meaning into my
body as I become the story you've been waiting for

But in the story you've been waiting for I will not be an I   and you will
not be a you   and for several minutes water will run toward me and it
will be the river of death and I will say no no it is not the river of death
it cannot be the river of death   but by the time I get the words out of my
mouth the river of death will have emptied itself out and the past will not
be the past and I won't know what it means to be dead

WHEN WILL I BE HUMAN AGAIN?

Apparatus #519

The part the whole the dead the corpse the foot the light the flesh
The wage
The worker
The regulator
The lie in the code of the body
It broke on the edge of itself
I did not trust what I knew was true
That my eyes were blank
That my face was blank
That my bone was blank
That my body was owned by the shareholders
That the body was just meat now
That the body was just debt now
That timedeath
Was murmuring so loud and I could only hear the dead rain
The squeak the buzz the machine
The breath the hatred the fumble the finger
The blow the key the sun the brain the bubbling
The cooling the box the space the fold
The silence the plank
I dropped all my capital in the supermarket
I was a young language with no verbs
I saw my stitches
Photographed from the inside
The police touched me frankly   so directly
They took me to
The mask the shield the armor the stone that's placed
On the grave
The body that's left in the ground
The mountain they moved to the city
The beach that sank in the city
The river that lost its water
The lake that lost its waves
The missing horizon the missing halo
The children that disappeared into the face of time
The tower the fire

The prose the sticks the woods
The foreclosed mountain we climbed before they threw us into
Another Wednesday another Tuesday another Monday
It's cruel to pray out loud cruel to pray
To a God who loves so
Discriminately
Cruel to eat in public
Cruel to sing when your neighbors can't speak moan or whisper to
The birth that refuses to drop
The death that refuses to rattle
The leg that refuses paralysis
Trust the hammer but lose the nail
Have faith in the hour but not the minutes
Don't speak the failed word the wound word
If it's witness to
The frozen the frosted the fickle the inspected
The inspector the hopeful the hopeless the crumbling the growing
The decaying the rooting the sowing the consuming
The fluid the formal the industrious
The callous the lazy the blank at the moment of blank
Be empty {again}
Disguise your breath
Disguise the sponge that sops up the water
Disguise the body that destroys its bones
The body that fears its own fingers
The concrete flesh
The privatized flesh
The bank flesh
The murmuring flesh
The murmuring blankness
The exhaustion
The suffering
The numbing
The weathering

I remember honey but it's gone now
I remember seeds but we have so few now
I remember the grass and the beach and the river

The bees and the ice
The lake and the mountain and its brokers
Its board members
Its collateral   its assets
Its insurance
Its expansion
Its reduction
We catalogued the glaciers before they disappeared
We returned the earth to the investors
The anxiety to the anxious
The babies to the umbilical cords
The blood to the state and the bank

Day #1101

The hospitals are exploding in the middle of the city and they tell us

The dead are not dead and the beach is disappearing

And the sand is disappearing and the lake and the dirty water and the children are disappearing

And the broken parents gamble with their own flesh because they know it has no value

They know their blood has no value   their hair has no value

And they ask the coroner

What can we bury here   there are so many bodies to bury

If we don't bury them soon

We will need to burn them or toss them into the river

And they ask the police

Are we allowed to mourn here

Has our request to mourn been stamped with the appropriate seals and signatures

Can the authorities confirm that we won't be

Immolated like the excess bodies   like the high schools

Like the sand and the lake and the patients who dissolve on the nightly news

Who char in the Bank of America

Can the authorities confirm whom we must pay

In order to mourn the bodies we love

The question is submitted through an encrypted browser

The question is submitted into the blankness of the bureaucracy

Thank you for your question   we will contact you as soon as

We locate an authoritative body

Who has been granted the permission to speak

But and

We need to thank someone because we have not yet been sacrificed like the sand

But and

We need to pay someone because we have not yet been disappeared like the sturgeon

We are not like the drinking water   we have not yet been   contaminated beyond repair

And we are still alive   though leaking with griefshame

And we are still broken   though dripping with griefshame

And our faces feel so hot because they are dying from so much life again

And our faces feel so hot because they are living from so much griefshame

We want to trade ourselves but we don't know

What we are worth to the operating system that controls the algorithms

That manage who we love   where we live   what we eat and whether or not

Our bodies will be blown into shards rubble ruins remains debris splinters

There is nothing to see here   say the authoritative bodies to the international observers

And it's true   our mouths are empty

Our eyes are empty

The price of my body is four

The price of my eye is five

The price of my future is twenty-two

There is no meaning for the depository

No rest for the depositor who is buried under the weight

Of the currency that ties him to a state that is not sovereign

There is no place for the weight of my thigh

I am hungry but there is no place for hunger

I am tired but there is no place for tiredness

Is my blood worth eighteen

Is my sperm worth fourteen

I have kidneys   I have a forceful face that does not know its place

I have a blank mouth that does not know what it can earn on the free market

And when I confess to what the authoritative bodies want me to confess to (that I live in the wrong body)

We learn that my life can't be verified among all the other lives

My four-digit codes are invalid

All of my passwords have vanished

Poem Written under a Pseudonym

—after Pedro Pietri

The play was written 104 years ago   but everyone who sees it says
sounds like it was written yesterday

The questions they asked back then about the boss and the debt and
the masses who are asses are just like the questions we ask now   she
says   only our questions are more complicated because back then
there weren't so many words that could be spoken in so many different
combinations   *know what I'm saying*

The dude at the skate shop (who in the dream is me) tells me (who in the
dream is also me) a long story about a dream he had where his mom (not
me) kept mistaking the word "invest" for the word "invent" and the word
"debt" for the word "death"

I pick up the pineapple and smell it through my mask and all the
shoppers in aisle twelve start laughing at me and someone whispers
"imagine if that pineapple were a machine gun" and someone else
whispers "imagine if that pineapple held inside of it everything you owe"
and someone else whispers "the Jewish fruit just doesn't get ripe here
anymore"

This reminds me of the day I couldn't get out of the bathroom because I
didn't want to be confronted with proof of my class condition

I publish my bad poems (the ones about debt and death) under a
pseudonym (daniel) but since I think my bad poems are actually my
good poems (the ones about the transience of ideology vis-à-vis the
permanence of nature) you might say I publish my best poems (the silent
ones) under a pseudonym (daniel)

According to the stage directions   the actors in the play are 104 years old

The first act is about a proletariat family who thinks using language to
communicate thought is a decadent relic of the bourgeoisie

(due to austerity measures   the play is only performed every 104 years)

The history of poetry is the history of bad poetry so you are always justified in publishing your worst poems under whatever damn name you please

The main characters get on a bus and when they sit down all the seats transform into babies and the audience thinks the babies are a metaphor for regeneration but when the bus breaks down in the middle of nowhere it becomes clear that the babies are a metaphor for death

He carries his belongings around with him on the bus after he is evicted from the commune in one of those epic battles between the Marxists and the Trotskyites

You think your poems don't matter at all and that no one reads them or cares about them then one day you get an email from a woman you've never met before telling you that her husband read your last book then killed himself and in the suicide note he keeps quoting lines from your poems and she thinks you should know this because you might want to take the book out of circulation to prevent others from having to bury the people in their lives they love most

Nationalism   democracy   dictatorship   the play within the 104-year-old play approaches these themes by forcing the audience members who are left-handed to stand in the corner and face the wall while the right-handed people study them from every possible angle of the universe   whispering *you and your debt are the same you and your debt are the same*

It's possible to pay back money with blood   says doctor #12347   If you know where to get the pure stuff you can make big money and disappear for a while into your own proper economy   the one where everybody knows that your rich and filthy name makes life more interesting than art again

That heart attack really saved my life   says character #10234.53a   the secret police were looking for me but luckily I was in the hospital having a tracheostomy

That's not you talking   it's the colonial axe in your head   the poem is
not real enough   the poem and the axe are the same

The talk show host was taking calls again about the horrors of urban
"pigeons"   his code word for poor people who "shit where they eat"   who
"eat wherever they please"

I'm not sure if I should give her a hug so instead I wave awkwardly and
thank her for writing my last few books for me

My favorite part of the play is when they arrest the woman who sells her
poems to poets on the black market (ghazals décimas Petrarchan sonnets
abecedarians and limericks for the kids)

Pigeon killing is a good issue to bridge party lines

The idealist in him wants to believe nonpartisan love affairs are still
possible among the bourgeoisie

She waives her copyrights and does not expect the poets to cite her when
they publish her best lines under their own names in the country's top
literary magazines

I'd rather not talk about race   he says   when your punctuation is just
so delightful

In my country   he says   when a baby is born   it's tradition to go out
into the street and shoot your gun into the air   to show gratitude to the
universe   for all it has provided

Sometimes fighting is useless   and it's best to give up   to say "uncle"   and
to wait for happier days

Performance of Becoming Human #418:
Excuse Me, Sir, What Time Is the Massacre?

welcome to the airbreathdeath theatre

here we are in   the airbreathdeath theatre

i drone away
        at my life in the airbreathdeath theatre

i drone away
        at my breathdeath in the airbreathdeath theatre

the episodes blast up like birds

the critics   like a coup of the imagination

the critics there to kill
        the coup of the imagination

the flowers fall flat on my head and the invisible body flings them from the
        balcony of the airbreathdeath theatre

I am dead in the morning
        of the airbreathdeath theatre

I am flat in the morning
        and there are so many books falling in the airbreathdeath theatre

they fall across the bodies of the dead

there are deserts in the mouths of the forgotten audience members
        in the airbreathdeath theatre

the mouths are like reduced mouths
        in the airbreathdeath theatre

we try to forget when we see the story
        of our breath moving backward in the airbreathdeath theatre

the translation of our breath
       moving   from side to side
           against the bodies that backtrack
               into the backstory of a backlife a backbeat

a refusal to move

       a refusal to translate

a refusal
       to make the breath
           knowable from one body to another
             from one tongue to another
               from one nation to another

the performance of becoming less human
       in the airbreathdeath theatre

aquí no hay epifanios   aquí hay puro silencio   y los cuerpos caen y caen

the movement from human to less human from humane to more humane
is not graspable

it runs mouth to mouth
it runs breath to breath
it runs death to death

it boils and runs and blooms and dies and forgets and revenges and robs
and runs and boils and runs and grows and forgets and revenges

and we   the performers in the airbreathdeath theatre
         build a life inside the ceremony of refusal
         the ceremony that begins with a little village-wiping bomb
         blast

the bombast

the bombed ass

the bomb in the bottom of history

la bomba en el culo del mundo

the body in the shamemouth of history

la bomba en la boca del cuerpo solitario

in the shaking hands in the exploding bodies

the death performers run with fear they run with frenzy

they airbreathdeath theatre into
                an unspoken desire
                                to reunite the self
                                        with the self
                                        the self with the other self
                                                the face with the other face

the grief with the collective grief the shame with the collective shame

desapareció la piña   desapareció el aguacate   las abejas desaparecieron
no hay un horizonte sobre el lago   no hay agua en la noche de petroleo

shame

how it dots the map

a colony of imperial dung

it dots the map it is

a colony of imperial dung

flung

from the mountain moaning in the middle of the city in the middle
of the empire in the middle of the shamemouth in the middle of the
airbreathdeath theatre

this is the road that leads to the airbreathdeath theatre

this is the road that hides a forgotten massacre

una gramática dolorosa no se mira en la boca

it is the road it hides a future forgotten massacre

it is a road it hides a resurrection it is a road

it hides the buckling of the earth the breaking of the pavement the collapsing of the highway

it is a road it hides a future massacre within a past massacre

is that a body or a mountain?

it hides a resurrection in the collective grief of the faces in the crowd

(excuse me, sir, what time is the massacre?)

no tengo confianza en esta traducción

they look blank   they are performing the mountainness of the mountain

the bodies in the airbreathdeath theatre are trying to become   the eternal
        embarrassment of nature

the disappearance of the most beautiful miserable valley has been captured
        in the faces of the audience at the airbreathdeath theatre

the captured orangutan turns human when none of the captors are looking

the audience members come to watch the disappearance of their own
bodies

they look out on the massacre road and see their bodies evaporating
(no surprise)

a documentarian photographs their faces stuck in the mountain

the economists celebrate the macroscopic potential of the animal's human transformation

the audience members are stuck in the resurrection of the collective grief

by the river the families weep with griefshame

and a voice sings backwards   i like the airbreathdeath theatre because it absorbs me

i like the airbreathdeath theatre   because it spits me out into a

a reduction of blankness

a reduction of epiphany

an innovation of extermination

a reduction of massacre

an innovation of resurrection

a reduction of performance

an innovation of extermination

a reduction of epiphany

a reduction in the blankness of blank

Lake Michigan, Scene #2022
{Nonessential Personnel}

they take our nonessential bodies to the lake and tell
us to record the history of the waves   the history of
the sand   the history of the wind   the history of the
horizon   the history of the snails and crabs   the lake
of disappearing bodies

they say   you must document the lake because we
don't know if it will be here tomorrow

and if it's not here tomorrow   then who is to say it
was ever here at all

they say   you are nonessential bodies   because
without you   the city will not disintegrate

but what they do not tell us is that soon   by necessity
we will become essential bodies   responsible for
containment   isolation   reinvention   documentation
simulation

we will become essential bodies who witness the
precise moment when the city transitions from
category one disaster to category two disaster to
category three disaster

we crawl with our heads pegged to the earth and
when we find bone or hair or torn clothing or bloody
bandages   we seal and store them as if they are
essential documents of western civilization

and when they ask us how the city will burn   we say
it will burn with God

and when they ask us about love   we say   love is
when we burn to save the lives of other bodies more
essential than our own

and we wonder   will it be essential or nonessential
personnel   who store us   who quantify us   who
protect us   who pay us and love us

will we be disassembled by essential or nonessential
bodies

we crawl to the lake and already we see its
disappearance

we look out into the distance and we understand that
after they burn the bodies   the sand and the lake will
disappear forever

and someone asks

where will your nonessential bodies go   when the
sand is gone

where will the water go   when the lake is gone

who will probe your voice   your skin   your hair   to
see if it is essential or nonessential

are the organs drying up in your body   essential or
nonessential

the essential blood documents of western civilization
are burning

the architecture in the intestines of the empire is
burning

the nonessential personnel are murmuring with
griefshame

the sand is shrieking its last shriek in the nonessential
archives of time

Writing #1209 {In the Penal Colony}

The writing is the knot that binds the gag

The writing is the bandage on the bleeding nose

The writing is the mouth that refuses to scream

The suppressed cough the scarred lip the shirt onto which the dribble is dripped

The air between observer and observed   between appraiser and appraised

This is the writing

The tongue that touches rope

Yarns   strands   fibers

The jaw that cracks backward

The finger that dies forward

The unfinished burn of the knuckle

The heavy creak of the floor

The red tint of the light bulb

The shifting of the shadow

The inverted mouth

The seconds cleaved into the eyes

The rancid milk at the bottom of the cup

The nail in the door and the shattered belt loop

The moment the appraiser looks away from the authentic body

The hybrid gland   the infected toenail

The excavation of the mouth

The discipline   the identification   the disappearance of molecular reality

If we can't write this then we can't write anything   he wants to say

But they need a report   an objective summation

They need to know how long it takes for the machine to inscribe its justice

They need to measure its power   its accuracy   its efficiency

Minutes hours volts watts gigabytes

The gentle hum of the authoritative machine

The impossibility of not looking at the digital display

Of not counting the seconds

Of not seeing the minutes

The screams that are screamed in the silence that can only be accessed
when it is understood that what must be documented   what must be
narrated   what must be evaluated   what must be written   is what can
never be documented narrated evaluated or written

What must be communicated is the indecipherability

Of a body that smiles when it is forced to smile

The curling of the lip is the writing

The wheezing of the lung is the writing

The sweat   the mucus   the ripped sock on the sweaty foot

The microscopic beings in the skin

The tiny hairs

The dead cells

The prose of the swollen jawbone

The moaning mouth is the writing

The writing is the breathscribble

The tonguescribble

The writing is

The word that will never arrive

WHEN WILL WE BE HUMAN AGAIN?

The Devouring Economy of Nature

The mark the skin the face the skin the bone
the skin the back the skin the reaping

the privatized face

the foreclosed back

the lake
was burning

the hedge fund
collapsing

too much liquid on the roof

too much debt in the face

too many bodies fleeing themselves

the bodies kept stepping out of their own
genetic mutations

kept forming new bodies

and when we tried to verify
what the old bodies meant
to the new bodies

we came to understand that the reason for the boiling heart

was that the storm was trying to make its way
out of the tax shelter

the raging hurricane was stuck
in the colony's backwater

the earth could not absorb
the colonial heat
the colonial wave
the crypto pump-and-dump

the rust the char the madness

the corpse's name carved into its skeleton

the photo they found in the corpse's pocket

the face they found in its pocket
the corpse they found in the bank

it was slick with oil

it was stuck
in the ceremony of bureaucracy
in the testimony of one bank head
saying to another bank head
no the people should not have
what we have
the people
if they are lucky   should have
what other people
in their tax bracket have

perhaps they can
ascend a bit
perhaps they can   slide
from side to side

there are bears waiting
to mop up the remains of the pump-and-dump

there are compliance officers
waiting

for the commission to declare
insufficient coverage in
the book the home the price the food the pipe the blood
the beating

the compliance officers filter the bodies
into a parallel superstructure
into a parallel pedagogy

the identity of the stuck body
floating or sinking

due diligence shows
the face is a vacancy

a pink sheet
a breath-note

a narrative of nature and nation
of what we might possess
when we   come to understand
how pain and time
are controlled   one by the other

the father said to his children

whose hands are these
and why have they
left them on our doorstep

whose feet are these
and why have they
placed them in our mailbox

I don't understand
what it is
they want from us

you see
we were living here
so quietly
then suddenly
our house was in another nation

and this is not a metaphor
the compliance officer said

and your house is not your house
for you have surely seen
the title
the deed
the language they found
in your basement

nevertheless

I understand you might prefer
to wait
for the bomb to crush your roof
said the nice functionary
to the bodies he needed to evict
but there is not always time
for such a grand gesture
of destruction

little by little
the bodies were repossessed
restructured

they were reinvented
transplanted
to the border
between disappearance and the absence of time

Day #429

the business of death is blooming the business of breath is blooming

the workers are covered from head to toe in disease

if there were more disease there might be less disease but since there is
not less disease there will be no disease or too much disease

we rub our bodies in bleach

we stick ourselves in cages

we don't know if we are in the present tense or the past tense

we see ourselves in parks   playing with children

there are soccer balls and goals and the lake is not the lake and the beach
is not the beach and in the middle of the city the streets are breaking
open but

this is not the apocalypse it is

normal to want to understand the difference between a body with

this much disease and a body with that much disease but today

the meat is infested the flour is infested the wheat is infested the grain is
infested the hand that touches the meat is

infested

the glove that slides onto the hand that touches the meat is

infested

I don't know what to say when everyone else is saying the same thing where to go when

I want to avoid the persistent murmur of time and death

this song used to be about a body lost in the desert

this song used to be about a boy trapped in a swimming pool with

fourteen economists who study him for profit for liability for exponential

growth for the ability to understand what

might happen when just a little body is reduced what

might happen when just a little face is reduced what

might happen when just a little weight is reduced just a snip of hair a trim
of skin a few fingernails a spit a swab a tooth a touch

are there different diseases are there different bureaucracies are there
different regulations are there different bodies who explode from too
much exposure to the day or the night or the solitude or the company
of others what do you know about the thing you love and how can you
know it is love but and

this isn't just a bad dream   but and

it's not just a stupid movie   but and

it's not just a battle between time and death between the rocks and the lake

between the water and the absence of water

between the lung and the breath

between the child and the body that births it

between the child and the body that loves it

between the mouth and the jaw that holds it

between the wind and the face that feels it

between the heart and the lips and all that you might forget when you die
again today and

all that you might remember when you die again today and

all that you might not know when you live again today and all that you
might not hear when you breathe again today

the disease sits between us and I cannot touch you anymore I

cannot see you except through a screen

I need to sleep for a very long time I only have five dollars I haven't had
lunch I

don't know where I can find flour

I don't know where I can find meat

everything I eat makes me sick

when the creditors call I will

pick up the phone and pretend I am happy to hear from them

I can't wait to give you my money I am so sorry I can't pay my bills so
sorry I can't pay the rent

so sorry I can't breathe through my mouth

I will miss myself so much when I die will you miss yourself so much

when you die will you miss me

when you disappear into the other language when you

disappear into the other silence when you

disappear into the other mouth when you

disappear into the other body

It is Day #429 and I need five dollars for lunch

I need bus fare

I need money for rent

I need to not be where I am

Sustainable Growth #205

What what what what   what do you cost

What what what what   what do you cost

How much how much how much   how much are they willing to give you

How much how much how much   how much are they willing to give you

What will you give them
What will you give them
What will you give them
What will you give

I will give them my face

       I need six dollars

I will give them my hand

       I need five dollars

My mouth is dead

I will give them something from my mouth

My mouth is dead

I need twenty-seven dollars for rice eggs bread milk

I'll sell my metadata for twenty-seven dollars

I'll sell you the metadata in the metadata of my metadata

What does my face cost?

       I need seven dollars for lunch

Metadata says I bought too many books about mental illness

What?

What does my condition cost?

I need to assess the metadata on my skin

How much for these knuckles?

How much for these ankles?

I will give them thirty-four hours a week   I will give them fifty-two hours
a week   I will give them 312 hours a month   I will give them twelve
hours a day   I will give them eight   forty-three   fifteen

Shhhhhh   Shhhhhh   Don't need to go to a third party for my metadata
I'll sell you my password   (Hr8491$what)

They test my metadata for toxicity

I have too many assets in my portfolio   but I don't own any of them

The assets are bloody

The assets are untimely

The assets are drowning

I look for my body but it's underwater
I look for my metadata but it's underwater
I look for my value but it's tied up in the metadata in my metadata

I look for my time but they tell me it's just a metaphor

I cannot interpret the metaphor unless I pay forty-six dollars

So many names for what I owe

Is your face really a surveillance machine that can hijack refugee data?

     So many things to put in my mouth

I have wrapped my head in double-grade fabric designed to block signal detection

     So many openings to fill with blank verse

     So many holes

     So many overpriced metaphors

I don't know where they put my body

Need less contaminated data need more unwavering data need more robust data

     Need to get the dead kids out of my data

I need six dollars for lunch

I need two dollars for the bus

I need five dollars to make it through the purge today

I cost more than I used to cost and less than my neighbors cost

I need a more precise assessment of my social relations

My exchange value needs to be corroborated

I need to know the most profitable body part to invest in

My house is underwater

I need to find the bridge

The bridge the boat the mouth the dirt the dollar

The judge says the state won't return my metadata until I can prove it won't be used for criminal activity

The value of my metadata is 400 dollars

I already paid 900 dollars in court fees and still I can't get my data back

I meet with a lawyer who says he can help me get my data back

We'll need some ripe organs   he says

I only have one decent kidney

What about antibodies?

The royalties on my antibodies were only thirty-seven dollars last year

He helps me unload some algorithms and I ask the judge to return my data baby

Judge says   you'll need to rehumanize your face before I let you touch that stuff again

I go back to the bank

They say my face can be exchanged for the future metadata of poor kids in developing countries who will soon be middle class

A banker tests my body for redundancies

He sends me to the vault for an appraisal

They take my DNA and I sign some papers I don't understand and the data analyst congratulates me

You are lucky   she says

You will always be human again

Responsory #0912

there is a path called overidentification with humanity

and on the path there is a line

and in the line there is a body within a body within a body that detains
all the other bodies

it prevents movement from one field of light to another

i remember sap and syrup   but they're gone now

i remember acorns and nettles   but they're gone now

come closer   i say to the depleted body

i need to listen to the cavity of your mouth   the cavity of your breath
the cavity of your knuckles

the body spits   and in the spit there are words that must be translated
from spit-language to language-language

the translator   all she can think of is capturing the spirit of the spit
the spirit of the piss   the spirit of the vomit   the things we value most
in our writing

they say we can distinguish between good death and bad death by how
the leaves smell

they say we can see the quality of the dying in the aromatics of the
deceased things trapped in a colony of action words

so many mass graves   says the poet   not enough time to write them

mother and child pose in front of the mass grave as the tour guide shows
them how they can best capture the experience   what angles to use so
the light will shine on the mass grave just so

the tour guide plays with the snakes and says now we must go to
the library where amid the bookshelves the death of the firstborn is
ceremonially followed by the death of the second-born the death of the
third-born   and so on

this   he says   is culture

but it might be a dream in which i am translating one of my most mundane
poems into a bestselling novel called *The Breathers* or *The Politics of Breath*
or *The Man Who Could Not Breathe*

it's a novel about the decadence of modernity

it wonders what would have happened if modernity had been a green bird
instead of a nuclear bomb

if modernity had been the islands and not the continent

if modernity were the opposite of debt and death

you see   i'm not particularly good with words

i don't have a big vocabulary

and i'd rather not speak of other bodies   but my writing-mouth-dream-
mind is filled with them

it's like that classic song   "I Try to Forget Things All the Time"

in the translation the song is called   "I Am Tripping Over My Lips to
Get to My Face"

scan the QR code and you'll hear the tune and see choreographed slips and
slides across the black box of wet and wild rhythms

time is a signal   says my therapist-lover   but what kind of signal is it
what kind of fungus is it   what kind of body is it

silence #243.423A or   the border between your body and mine

they say the international frontier is just a gesture   but the border-
crossing "mice" know it is infinite   they know the world as a series of
lines you cannot cross   a series of limbs you cannot articulate

in other words   comma

the splintered finger   at the end of this poem   is nothing more than

a splintered finger at the end of a poem

you see it and you don't see it

what do you think about when your body is being "thrown out quickly"

they chisel the gold out of my teeth only to find a plastic bag   a knife and
a poem   infinitely emerging from the body of a slaughtered soldier

Lake Michigan, Scene #525

The hunger

The lake of the disappeared

So many maniacal fathers   so many cops   so many cannibals

On Lake Michigan   the teenagers weep the disease of the unitedstatesian night and comfort each other when the cops aren't obstructing the end of this shithole absence

The thread that connects the boys to the sky and the earth and the planets

The tenderness of one boy embracing another

The tenderness of one human being loved by another

The boys sing

We are nothing to the galaxy and we are nothing to our city

The maw of human perception   desperation   survival

When night turns to day and day turns to night and night turns to day

The boys become

Bodies made of disease

Bodies made of a love they do not have

Bodies made of all the love they have

Bodies that are just bone

Rotting bodies

Shrinking bodies

Bodies that screech alone and break alone

Today the boys dream the police are not torturers

They dream their fathers can unlearn the violence baked into their bodies when they were children

The impressionable bodies

How if you press on them

You will leave a clear mark

A scar   a knife wound   acid burned into the flesh of the refusing body

We listen to the wind on the lake and it is like a prayer we sing when we are sick of being alive but are too afraid to die

When we do not want to continue   the cycle of sickness and decay

We have to eat   one way or another

We have to survive   one way or another

The mothers are kept out of the narrative

But in their absence

We sense the oracular

We sense our own births as existing

In the diseased flesh of the shithole nation

How much consciousness will grow in the dead tree

How many cities will spill out of the dead lake

The animal stands before the oven

It does not know it should be sad   in the face of its own obliteration

Beloved is

The wretched body that refuses to die

The mouth that won't open

The voice that won't speak

The tooth that won't chew

The authoritative body says

Don't be hungry if you're near the market

Don't be poor if you're near the rich

Don't let them see the house they built from your bones

Beloved is

The overpriced hour

The unaffordable minute

The day that can't be bought

Beloved is the CEO of the water

His accountants

His attorneys

His ownership of life and death

WHEN WILL YOU BE HUMAN AGAIN?

There is nothing to do
For our liberation,
except wait in the horror of it

   John Ashbery

There is nothing to do
For our liberation,
Except wait in the horror of it

   John Ashbery

but they say *you owe nothingness*

   Roque Raquel Salas Rivera

There is nothing to do
For our liberation,
except wait in the horror of it

   John Ashbery

but they say *you owe nothingness*

   Roque Raquel Salas Rivera

but they say *you owe nothingness*

   Roque Raquel Salas Rivera

There is nothing to do
For our liberation,
Except wait in the horror of it

   John Ashbery

but they say *you owe nothingness*

   Roque Raquel Salas Rivera

(Excuse me, sir, what time is the massacre?)

****** is for the dead *******   ******* is for the dead *******

The living for the ★ ★ ★ The living for the ★ ★ ★

Insert Bodies Here

He gets in the way of a bullet
The city floods
He gets in the way of a bulldozer
The state groans
He gets in the way of a machine gun
He hears someone say
It's none of your business how many people we must save from
       themselves
The highway is blocked
Supplies can't get through
He hears someone say
It's your choice, you get to decide how much pain you want to feel
A building crumbles
A bed fills with blood
A voice says
You get to decide how much the tumor will grow
A girl starves
The lake overflows
The trucks can't get through
No rice no bread no drinking water
A voice says
You get to decide how far you will fall
A soldier appears
He is also an artist
He talks to a journalist
I feel something "complex" about the human rights abuses I have committed
The journalist assumes he means the human rights abuses
       he committed in a third world shithole
But really he means
The human rights abuses he committed here in the shithole of Chicago
A boat fills with refugees fleeing Illinois and Indiana
A boat fills with refugees trying to get to Canada
The water calms
The sun rises
A prison is built out of twigs and branches
It fills up with destitute immigrants

The artist-soldier shoots himself in the head, his best performance
No one watches
A police officer asks to see our papers
We only have toilet paper
You need to apologize for getting in the way of our bullets, he says
You need to stop letting us torture you
The police officer beats us a bit
You only have toilet paper and not even that can keep your asses clean
He laughs and beats us a bit
He asks for our numbers
No numbers
He asks for our names
No names
He asks if we can measure the economic impact of our bodies in Molotov
    cocktails
Windows shatter
Several dogs are reported as casualties
A poet appears on the scene
A vulture appears on the scene
The poet and the vulture search for the form of the apocalypse
Why do you keep getting in the way of our bullets
The form mutates
Institutions dissolve
The town radiates, glows pleasantly
The mayor gets angry
The teachers lose their pensions
The land swallows some bodies
The prison is on fire
I am limited by my intuition
I am limited by my constitution
I am limited by my indiscretion
I am limited by my access to nuclear waste
The land explodes gently
The system breaks down then regenerates
A momentary sense of triumph
I see snakes on the road
A momentary sense of triumph
I see rabbits on the road

Bees return to the city
A child is struck in the head with a battery
The whole country flows out of a dead man's mouth
Some babies are born
Refugees keep coming from Kansas
The police want to know what color they are
The Kansans don't know what color they are
The police officers guess what color they are
They look pinkish or mauve or ochre
Someone wants to interrogate their outer layers
A philanthropist has a suggestion
Maybe we can bury them in that pretty little hole?
Words keep appearing: disease, dehydration, hospitalization
A priest and a rabbi walk into Target
That's no priest, that's an alley
That's no alley
That's another child who needs to apologize for getting in the way of our
       bullets
The Bank of America bursts into flames
Money flows out of a dead man's mouth
Insert bodies here

Performance of Becoming Human #1025:
The Police or the Bank of America

We are in the airbreathdeath theatre   waiting for the massacre to begin

And he says your uncle   your uncle Mauricio   what does it mean that
he killed himself after he threw all the money in the river

And I say no no he didn't kill himself   on the contrary it was only after
he threw all the money in the river that he was able to keep living

I want to say something profound about the permanence of nature in
relation to the transience of human life

But my tongue won't move in the right direction and the bourgeois
barbarian keeps asking me what does it mean what does it mean

What does it mean that he throws money into the river

What did money ever do to him

What will he do in a world without money

What does it mean that your uncle could not differentiate between his
own skin and martial law

What does it mean that he does not know the difference between his
kidney and a power line

What is suicide week

Who killed themselves on suicide week

What do you mean when you say his mouth was filled with bullets

What did the bullets taste like   Did they really taste like orgasms

What does the electricity jolting out of your uncle's neck mean to you

What does this darkness mean to you

I whisper   I can barely get the words out of my mouth

I murmur   *the police*   is what it means to me

Everything I write is because of the police

I hate the police outside my body and I hate the police inside my body

All I ever wanted is to keep the police away from the outside of my body
and keep the police away from the inside of my body

I can barely say the words   I am whispering in the airbreathdeath theatre
about the police

That's what it means to me

I was trying to keep the police out of my poem

I was writing to keep myself from policing my poems

I was writing to ward off the police   inside my body and outside my body

Writing was like a prayer

If I kept writing

If I never spoke to anyone   I say

Perhaps the police would never bother me

I was wrong   of course

The police officer moved into the apartment downstairs then I found
out he killed a boy in an alley and I couldn't sleep at night because I was
terrified

As I tried to sleep I kept seeing the police officer downstairs shooting the boy in an alley

The police officer would lift weights in the yard behind our building and I could hear him grunting from exertion

He killed a boy in an alley and he also won multiple fitness awards from the Chicago Police Department

Sometimes I had to walk by him as he was lifting weights and grunting and I was terrified and wanted to tell the entire building he had killed a boy in an alley

But I did not tell the entire building because I realized my neighbors would not care and many of them felt safer because there was a police officer in the building

I did not feel safer

On the contrary   I felt less safe and I was angry and scared and to deal with my anger and fear I wrote a poem about "my uncle" (in reality this character was much more like me than my uncle) who killed himself because he could no longer live in a world with police and money

I am whispering all of these things in the airbreathdeath theatre and the bourgeois barbarian hates me with every bone in his body

Excuse me sir   I ask him   shaking   when will the massacre begin

But he doesn't hear my question and I ask him again   what time is today's massacre   and he hears me now but he refuses to answer and instead he keeps asking me what it all means

The police   he says   what do they mean to you

Property   he says   what does it mean to you

The earth the state the bank   what do they mean to you

And I tell him that every poem I write is a poem about the police or the bank and that every book I write should be called *The Police* or *The Bank of America*

All I have ever wanted in the shallow ravine of the airbreathdeath theatre is to write book after book called *The Bank of America*

And he spits at me and asks me about the timeline

I need to know   he says   when will you be human again

I need to know   he says   if you understand the implications of your inaction

I need to know   he says   what it means to you when you see the earth dissolving

When you see sand in the sky

When you see sky in the wrong place

When you see nuclear waste in the river

When you see your tongue in the wrong mouth

What does any of it mean to you

I feel so much pressure to speak   but I have nothing to say

And so I breathe   I just breathe and think about breathing as the bourgeois barbarian asks me to explain the meaning of my hungry body

He screams   why is your face so blank

Surely it must mean something that your eyes are so dirty and blank

What does it mean that your words are so blank

The limping dog licking the broken face in the ruins

What does it mean to you

The starving child eating garbage in the ruins

What does it mean to you

The bloodwords in the statemouths

The poetry of the shattered bone that keeps breaking so beautifully in the atrium of the airbreathdeath theatre

What does it mean to you

The diseased water   the diseased breath   the diseased lung

What does the justification mean to you

What does the rationalization mean to you

Just breathe   I tell myself   Just breathe

Hello again from the airbreathdeath theatre

Excuse me sir   I really need to know   what time is today's massacre

The breath performers in the airbreathdeath theatre keep telling me to breathe

The death performers in the airbreathdeath theatre keep begging me to breathe

There is your uncle on the bridge   says the bourgeois barbarian
when he throws money into the river

What does it mean

How long   he says   do you plan to be beast

What is the timeline for your transformation   he says

When will you be human again

Lake Michigan, Scene #1130

A cop / is standing / on every corner of the universe
(Pablo de Rokha, tr. Urayoán Noel)

the water disappeared and the sand disappeared
and the dunes disappeared into the carcass of the
unitedstatesian night

the city disappeared and the state disappeared

no one knows where the trees are

no one knows where the birds are

no one knows if the story is about a body that's dead or
missing or sleeping

we look out at the blankness and see the lake even
though the water is not there

we see the waves in the water that is not there

we see the city opening up out of the water that is not
there

Chicago emerges from the disappeared waves and
in the distance we see the borders of the dead states
rising from the sand that is not there

the dunes have crumbled but we remember how as
children we climbed them with thirst and desire
and joy

we remember who we were before the perch and trout
disappeared   once they had tasted good but now we
feel sick from the bacteria swarming in the petroleum
of our stomachs

the factories are still here but no one cares for them

the workers are still here though mostly they've been dumped into the torso of the carcass economy

we look out at the blankness where once there was lake and we imagine new states forming on the horizon

Indiana and Michigan are absorbed by the privatized waves

the CEOs of the water ask us to forgive them and we say it is not in our power to forgive

we see the history of our bodies cracking open once more in the middle of the blankness of the lake

the corpse of the continent opens up in the magnetosphere and in the changed particles of the solar wind

and when the parliamentary slag heap forms out of the blankness of the lake

we understand that the tradition of justice and the tradition of injustice are simply bodies that break and heal   like the rest of us

they are ghosts dispersed through the undergrowth of this country that can't stop burning

where time has been overproduced   where history has been overproduced

we look to the south and see the skyscrapers blooming out of the thirsty city

we look to the north   toward the occupied territories
of Wisconsin   and see the cops standing on every
corner of the universe

blessed are the constellations of growling children

blessed are the daisies that form in their eye sockets

blessed is the water that's missing

blessed is   the water to come

Secret Code #306

A drunk poet in the audience heckles me   *You're not as good as Artaud*   he yells   *You'll never be as good as Artaud*

He apologizes after the reading and asks me if I like Artaud

I tell him my opinions about Artaud and he suggests we meet for coffee

The headline of the article reads "Chicago Poet Seized as Fugitive Killer"

She kisses me and says   *I only like you for your exchange value   no one cares about your use value*

The fugitive poet didn't appear to have a violent side he was an antiwar activist and everyone thought he was funny

When I was younger   I was taught that curiosity about the secret code would inevitably lead to catastrophe

They say you can only understand your own body after you have understood the bodies of others

The boys have a problem   their fathers   they want to solve the problem by killing them

I only use punctuation to convey confusion?   or enthusiasm!

All the words make sense   I understand the text   the subtext   the connotations   the metaphors   the references and allusions   but in the end I have no idea what any of it actually means

I ask her for her password and she whispers in my ear
Bearwolf43!

When he was a child he believed he could change a
thing by looking at it

If I don't see it does it actually exist?

I spent two years writing a poem called "The
Destruction of the Global Economy" It's about a bank
that has so much money it actually has no money at all
It's about a man who buys 100 houses and sells them
for 125 percent profit   It's about the way in which
the bank loans money to both the man who sells the
houses and the people who buy the houses and when
the people who buy the houses can no longer afford
their loans the bank sells the houses back to the man
who buys the houses and he sells them again to people
who cannot afford the houses

(Insert analogy about   the push and pull of the broken
body)

I thought it was a good poem but I've never shown it to
anyone and now it sounds stale and outdated

In my head I say over and over again *Bearwolf43!*   but
when it comes time to type in the password the animals
have escaped me   *Beowulf43!   Baywatch43!*

It's not a bad idea to learn how to build a ventilator

I want to believe that if I look at the television long
enough I might change the outcome of the game

My father calls with an urgent message: *the market
doesn't care about your feelings!*

You can begin a sentence in the middle of another sentence in order to make a new sentence

Care about your feelings!

You can write the sentence as if the subject were implied or you can write the sentence as a question

It doesn't care about your feelings! Doesn't it care about your feelings?

I ask about the secret code and she tells me it's an ever-changing set of unarticulated knowledge that I am too uncouth to access

You can take classes on etiquette   you can hire a professional to manage your skin care and hygiene you can subscribe to a service that buys clothes for you

I own six pairs of jeans but I wear the same ones every day

The man who builds 100 houses says   *Some people call me a successful entrepreneur   Others call me a capitalist scumbag pig   It all depends*   he says   *On the words you like to use to describe your relationship to living*

I can't focus on the movie because I keep thinking of snappy responses I could have said to the poet who tells me I will never be as good as Artaud

I'm sick of being alive but I'm too afraid to die

(is it okay if I tell you this?)

You can look into the sky and see a thread that connects your body to the planets and the stars

I don't know what that means   but I suspect it might
be true

What is the name of that tree?

Day #1103

That we cannot move our securitized feet
That we cannot move our private hands
That we cannot move our debt-filled fingers
There is light in our debt-filled fingers
There is light in our securitized feet
Money makes the light turn from orange to yellow to purple
The embarrassment of nature
The light that blazes in the fingers we do not own
The fingers in the body of us all

The body of no one
The foam in the hand of the suffering lake
The crisis-lake in the hand of the performer becoming human
The lord-becoming-human in the hand of the fictional bank
I am floating in the fluorescent lake foam
without feeling

I don't know the name of the contamination
I don't know the identity of the sludge

I don't want
I don't ask
They don't see me

Dot Dot Dot Dot Dot Dot Dot

Period

End stop the light end stop the movement

End stop the song we sing to the blasted bodies we don't know

End stop the song we sing to the privatized bodies we don't hear

We sing it to the broken bodies we don't want to become

We sing it to the bodies we hurt the bodies we
frame the bodies we bake the bodies we smoke
the bodies we paint the organs we cannot pay for

Our liver we deposit
How much does it cost

Our kidney they loan us
How much does it cost

The labor
The interest
The ratio of debt to asset

I don't know what to do I need a few dollars

I need four I need five I need four I need
another dollar I need to pay the debt I owe
on my organs what are they willing to take what
are they willing to give me in exchange for myself

Bank says I cost too much

Bank says I cost too little

Bank says I must repeat life   again

Bank says the strongest part of me

Has already been foreclosed upon

So gently
like a sweet little burden
The debt drops
It hears us
So gently
It translates our griefshame
Into

The poem of the broken lung
The poem of the broken bed under the drowning nation
The poem of the drowning nation that lives beneath another drowning nation

The lake and the beach are closed
again

The sand and the geese have disappeared
again

Thirty-six people died here today

Sing the authoritative bodies

Tough break folks

An unforeseeable act of nature

WHEN WILL THEY BE HUMAN AGAIN?

Utopia 527–528

527

Beloved   we saw a death machine

And its manual read

Press this button to detect bodies carrying drugs across the border

We saw another death machine

And its manual read

This machine is appropriate for detecting small-scale and large-scale international border crossings

We blew up the machines

And a radio wave measured the composition of our blood as we invaded a gated community with forty-three houses and forty-three swimming pools

And in one house

Dozens of our finest hackers were dismantling global trade networks resignifying the tools the entrepreneurial classes had created to enhance the flow of capital

And a CEO said

If everybody catches a deadly disease   then who will buy our products

And a CEO said

If everybody catches a deadly disease   then what will be the meaning of love

And the CEO was deported with a busload of hedge fund managers and bankers

And the police were destroyed with aluminum phosphide

And ICE was destroyed with liquid termiticide

And we moved back and forth across the border

As swiftly as tax-free commerce

528

Beloved were

Our immigrant parents who sold stocks and derivatives on their smart phones

They owned retirement funds and timeshares and SUVs

And they did no labor to obtain them

And they placed little value upon them

And they were liberal in giving

And liberal in taking

And liberal in eating and sleeping and publishing and fucking

And a voice said

What right do you have to tell your story

And our parents took out their medical records   which verified   they had suffered enough trauma   to not have to worry about   New York publishers concerned with the marketability of their authenticity

And the border patrol agents were stuffed into boxes with thousands of cellular phones

As they were smuggled out of the occupied territories of Arizona Texas and New Mexico

And we gave them water to drink

And the water was good

And the water was pure

(And the water was owned by Coca-Cola and Nestle and an unnamed conglomerate of stakeholders in China Qatar and Germany)

And we harvested melons and strawberries

And consumed blue jeans and cellular phones and plasma TVs

As we birthed hundreds of thousands of unitedstatesian babies

Whom we dressed in indestructible onesies

Sewn from protein-based fabrics   that can never ever catch fire

There is comfort in touching yourself to make sure
you're alive

I try not to look at my phone in bed but I can't resist
I'm afraid of missing out

I understand your pain   he says   my body is a veritable
catastrophe

Dark and cryptic   practical yet idealistic

If I describe myself this way will she still want to date
me?

You can formulate a vision of a society not destroyed
by colonialism and capitalism   but it's best to keep it
to yourself

After she died we discovered my grandmother kept a
journal of all the food her family members liked

I find my name next to a note that says   *hates bananas
loves smoked gouda*

Her parents find her diary and punish her when they
learn she smokes pot and has sex with her boyfriend

The CEO goes on television to tell the shareholders
they should not expect rewards in the short-term

The next day there is a major sell-off and the price of
the stock drops 15 percent

The day after everyone buys the stock at a discount
and soon it hits all-time highs

That's the least you can do when so many people are dying

The thrill of keeping a diary is knowing someone will surreptitiously read it

We keep waiting for the price to drop but it never does

He asks her what's left of her country

There's nothing but blood and skeletons

Some people think resilience is more important than education

I feel sick to my stomach when I think I've spent too much money

The punch line of the joke is   *here, take my husband!*

You can give a kid a good school or you can teach her to successfully adapt to the reality that she'll never get to go to a good school

I start laughing at jokes before the teller even finishes telling them

I tell the doctor   *it feels like two ghosts are having sex in my body*   he takes notes and never looks up

I do math problems in my head to help me fall asleep

There's blood in the bathwater and I don't know who it belongs to

I only live here because it's a tax haven   free from regulatory oversight

The sign on the door says   *The emergency will never end*

The joke begins   *I bought my husband a wooden leg for Christmas*

It takes several decades to discover that his failing kidneys are the result of too much arsenic in the drinking water of his childhood home

He can't find a word as ugly as   *gastroenterologist*

I've never said the phrase   *I'm as naked as the day I was born*

The poet asks the audience to take off their clothes and lie belly down on the ground with their hands across their heads

If you're poor you shouldn't take your citizenship too literally

Whose woods these are I think I know

That's all I remember from high school

Lake Michigan, Scene #131

I cannot hold on I see myself shrinking.
I see the waves absorbing us. They are so
much kinder than the sinking city. The
waves want us. The collapsing city does
not. It spits us into the screaming basin.
An authoritative body asks us how much
grit we need to survive the dormant
police-state-austerity-regime. We are
drowning. We are searching for light.
We are searching for posthumous
sincerity but all I can hear is the broken
testimony, the poetry of the infected
lung. The poetry of the drowning mouth.
The raw bits of shithole life that keep
crumpling up in the wastewater. And the
lake foam is like plastic justice. The foam
is an amorphous cage. It is the bluff, the
code, the last verb she spoke before she
was tossed into the privatized sinkhole.
The privatized sand is weeping. The
privatized lake is petroleum (again). It is
gurgling. It is exploding. It is asking us
to follow the route it has established.
This way to the end of your amorphous
privatized cage. This way to the wound-
channel the earth cannot swallow. And
we dance this way. And the lake vomits
out its God-waste this way, vomits up
the oil-slicked sturgeon, the rattling
death-breath of millions and billions of
minnows. We fight for our bodies and we
hope for a quiet battle. We do not want
to die alone and we pray for invisible
consolation. We do not covet the
protections they do not offer us.

How I Wrote Certain of My Books

I met the poet before he disappeared

The timeline of events doesn't make sense

I don't think you are lying but I suspect there are gaps   elisions
important details you are not disclosing

You have a way of speaking that doesn't allow me to ask questions

Are you like this with everyone?

You keep the people who love you most at a distance   drawing them
in when they talk about themselves yet holding back when they want to
know more about you

I met the poet in a writing workshop he offered out of his home

I was one of four students in the class

There was one student who never spoke and never turned in any writing
and the poet loved her because the silent student understood that the
ultimate form of poetry was silence and we all saw something sublime
in her refusal to acknowledge even the most basic forms of communal
norms and discourse

Another student was a father of three kids

He owned a small business and was "doing something for himself for
a change"

Austerity measures have forced me to abandon aesthetic or narrative
unity

I work too much and I don't have time to write anymore and it limits my
creativity and coherence

I cut my budg by twenty-five perc and now I can't eve finis a

The poet's preferred way of signing books was   *Greetings from the land of
anti-value*

Like all good poets the poet hated his own poetry

I loved his first book but he thought all the poems were cheap imitations
of René Char and Gertrude Stein

All poets should hate their own poetry   said the poet

You should never be able to look at your own poetry without feeling
utterly repulsed

If you are proud of your own poetry or enjoy reading your own poetry
then you need to figure out how to write poems that will offend yourself
just a little bit more "robustly"

The father of three who was doing something for himself for a change
wrote epic poems about his childhood

The poet referred to the father of three's poems as sociopathic imitations
of Frank O'Hara   only more interesting

They were horror stories   frankly   and none of us knew how to respond
to them

The poet loved that we didn't know how to respond to the father of
three's poems

He thought the best response to a poem was to feel like what the fuck did
I just read I don't have a fucking idea what I just read what did I just read
do you understand remotely what I just read what the fuck am I reading

And it appeared that the father of three met this standard of what-
the-fuckery in his epic poem about a man (now a poet of course) who
watched his mother kill his father when he was a child

Did the father of three's mother actually kill his father?

(Fuck you said the father of three I'm not telling)

Probably not but every once in a while his poems would contain the kind of detail   a line from a coroner's report or a snippet from a newspaper article that led us to think that something along those lines must have happened

The father of three was kind and cheerful and always showed up to the workshop with wine or cookies or cake

The poet would give advice like   fuck doing new things   you're a writer not an *iPhone*

You don't need a constant update

You don't need to keep changing your algorithm

The other student in the workshop was an attorney and she was about to retire

Her favorite poets were H.D. and Sylvia Plath and she knew almost every detail of Greek mythology, which often served as tropes in her poems

She wrote poems that possessed what the poet once called "a subtle hint of bureaucratic eroticism"

She was terrified of retiring and was "pursuing" poetry because she wanted to make sure she had plenty of activities to keep her mind from atrophying in her retirement and so she designed complex mazes of poems that were impossible to work their way out of and the poet would ask her questions like

What does this poem hate? What does this poem love? How can you make this poem hate more lovingly and love more hatefully?

I was the other student in the workshop and I hated writing poems that looked like poems so the poet thought I had the right attitude about poetry even if my poems were didactic or bland or facile

It's not that I'm a bad writer   the critic wrote about my last book   rather I appear to be writing as a bad writer on purpose

I never thought of myself as being a bad writer on purpose but as soon as the critic said this a light bulb went off   *I must think of myself as being a bad writer on purpose*   and then everything changed   I wrote a bad book on purpose and it was the best book I ever wrote and I won a big prize and I was invited to give a reading at Harvard

I am flexible and I mold my so-called aesthetic choices to satisfy the criteria of the basest members of my audience

The poet didn't know if being a poet meant being the best/worst version of himself or the best/worst version of someone else

The object of a poem   he used to say   is to try to put every possible thing into the poem so that the poem is not so much a poem but a container for the entire world and in this way there might eventually be no distinction between living and writing and art and life and art and death and the world as we know it and the world we desire and the world we despise

Unitedstatesians are obsessed with privacy   Is that your chocolate in my peanut butter?

Every line I've ever written is a version of another line I've ever written and sometimes I write the same lines over and over again to see if they sound different in a different context

As a child I spent fourteen hours a day watching television

Is that your chocolate in my peanut butter?

They say the poet went crazy but it was just back spasms that triggered a series of medications and hallucinations which led to him being admitted into a psychiatric hospital named after a nineteenth-century war criminal

Is a bear Catholic?

Does the pope shit in the woods?

He classified my poem as a bad imitation of Vicente Huidobro's "Monumento al Mar"   but in reality it was nothing like Huidobro or perhaps it was a bit like Huidobro if Huidobro wrote about psychoanalysis death metal   the television show *Twin Peaks*   a device to detect drugs hidden in the gastrointestinal tracts of border crossers   the unspoken relationship between Moses and his more talkative brother Aaron Kafka's short story "A Report to an Academy" and getting your cell phone stolen while stepping out of the metro in downtown Santiago on your way to lunch at a restaurant that used to be in the house where Vicente Huidobro lived as a child

I recognize that some readers will feel alienated by a reference to a poem they haven't read by a writer they haven't read but I'm not choosy or pretentious and mostly I believe that words and names are interchangeable

I like the flow of your poem but I have no idea what any of it actually means

He classified my poem as a bad imitation of Emily Dickinson's *Hope is the thing with feathers* yet he told me I did such a good job of writing a bad imitation that he could not forego giving me the highest possible marks on the assignment

A phrase as simple as "I hate your fucking guts" can mean a thousand different things to a thousand different people

It was the end of a long evening and the poet was feeling generous so he gave me a thumb drive with decades' worth of unpublished writing   a memoir   a novel   three or four collections of poems   and told me to do whatever I want with them

I'm dying frankly and I think it would be great for your career if you put
your name on some of the better poems and sent them out for publication

According to brittanica.com there is a form of torture called "Crushed by
Elephant" which is when a prisoner is placed on the ground in front of
an elephant and crushed by it

But I'm warning you   if you google "Crushed by Elephant"   you will
feel as if the entire internet already knows that people have been crushed
by elephants for centuries   and it might be more beneficial to search for
"scaphism"   the ancient practice of a sealing a victim between two boats
feeding him milk and honey   covering his face with milk and honey so
that flies swarm around his face   and then   as the victim defecates
inside the boat   flies and maggots "grow up inside" and slowly devour
his flesh

Now that the country is "teetering on dictatorship" the poets have
come to believe that the subjectivity of subjective experience has a
responsibility to be as ugly as the objectivity of objective experience

Awkward sentence bro

Time for another revision

Disaster Exposure

You ask him if his hedge fund has sufficient exposure
to disaster and he whispers

I could really use a hurricane to deliver   superior fund
performance

What do *you* see that other people cannot see?

Everything in this poem is on the surface   there is no
subtext or subtext to the subtext   the words only mean
what I want them to mean

I am not so interested in the imagination   and I am
more than capable of exploiting disaster concerns to
deliver superior fund performance

Tell the story a different way

The doctor says   *Patient cannot tell the difference
between what he is and what he owes*

Describe the aesthetics of the disaster

Every collapsing system is a poem in itself

Lucky for me   I am paid by the syllable to write it

You ask him if his disaster risk is heterogeneous and
he says   *All you need is a touch of disaster exposure and
you will see a beautiful increase in the returns on your fear
premium*

But seriously boss

How bad does it have to be before we can call it a
disaster

How broken does your body need to be before we can
call it a disaster

He dithers

She dithers

They dither (this is dithering)

Tell the story a different way

The interest in your body is the origin of your world

It all begins with a credit default swap

A complex financial product whose name sounds like
a natural mineral

(Baby I love it when you say   *Superior Fund
Performance*)

Let's do some quick math on the quote-un-quote back
of this envelope

There are hundreds of lost bodies and thousands of
lost limbs

Are they enough?

The river is in the wrong place again

Is that enough?

The highway is hanging from the mountains again

Is that enough?

The mountains are covered with rooftops

The electric pole has been in the middle of the road for so long that people have confused it for a work of art

But and

The disaster that surrounds us is not really a disaster

But and

You begin with debt   and you end with debt   and when there is no debt   you don't know what to do because all you have ever known is debt

SUSTAINABLE GROWTH

a book sprouted behind,
over the corpse, abruptly

    César Vallejo

The dead always died from life

    César Vallejo

I shall miss myself so much when I die

    Clarice Lispector

I shall miss myself so much when I die

    Clarice Lispector

a book sprouted behind,
over the corpse, abruptly

    César Vallejo

The dead always died from life

    César Vallejo

Excuse me, sir, what time is the massacre?

We Are in the Future Now!

I dreamt I was baking an apple pie and in the dream I woke up and you said: *Your dreams are so good I can smell them.*

They shot some _____ *last night. No one knows how many* _____ *died. We are saddened by this senseless loss of* _____.

When I speak to you sincerely, it may seem like I'm talking about mercy. But everyone knows that in Chicago "dying" is not the same as "dying."

~~What does capitalism have to sell you that you haven't already sold to yourself? (sic!)~~

I was thinking about the old cliché: the one where the starving man peels off his skin and eats himself then gets indigestion because he ate so fast and didn't drink enough water.

Whiny journalists always asking questions like: *How many people died here yesterday? How many corpses did they burn?*

Revolution or brunch? Not as simple as it sounds

They say it's okay to enjoy things when the world is exploding. I'm not so sure I believe them.

The police-state-austerity-surveillance-machines stopped spying on themselves when they realized the only step left was to report their own bodies to the censors.

And the bureaucrats sing: *We are in the future now! We are in the future now!*

I don't really care for any of the years, decades, or centuries. I don't like states, countries, or nations. And I'm not a fan of time, religion, justice, culture, literary movements, schools of painting or philosophy, "the commons," "the archives," semantics, rhetoric, politics, the ego, the id, the public self, the private self, oratory, syntax, or grammar, among other things.

The history of this road is   Massacre A then Massacre B expansion peace treaty truth reconciliation resurrection   Massacre C then Massacre D   rhetorical guilt legal challenges truth reconciliation hypocrisy Massacre E then Massacre F.

Period.

You can have an inspiring "studio session" in Emily Dickinson's bedroom in Amherst for $300 for one hour, or $500 for two hours. Or two people can rent it out for $400 for one hour, or $600 for two hours. Food and drink must be left outside the room. The door will remain open. Staff will be present at all times.

At *Sophie's Choice: Custom Gifts and More* in Niagara Falls, you can buy a maternity shirt that says "Expecting our first lil' Pumpkin." At *Sophie's Choice Shop,* an online retailer servicing Serbia, Montenegro, Croatia, Bosnia, and Herzegovina, you can buy makeup and fake eyelashes. At *Boutique Le Choix de Sophie* in Alma, Quebec, you can buy "everything for your wardrobe from head to toe." At *Sophie's Choice Clothing,* an online secondhand shop from the UK, you can buy tunics, strappy dresses, and fashionable outfits for the office.

When he said I was "asleep at the wheel" what I thought he meant was that I was "sleeping on the side of the road" which I thought of as "dying on the side of the road" or even just "sleeping on the side of death."

Best Practices #1013

She pulls out her passport and the agent says   your
country no longer exists

We tread lightly over the broken bones so we won't
cause them to explode or decay

He wants to know the name of this atrocity so he can
classify it among the previous ones

We dig deeper into our faces to find the acceptable
calculations that might alter the course of history (is it
too soon to embellish the dead?)

Time passes   Nothing changes   The hours become
worse and worse

There is a militarized frontier in your face and you
cover it with the sixty-four-digit code that all the
miners are searching for

We can't advance until we know the name of this
period of infinite gestation

They need to build a system whose death leads to the
most efficient form of regeneration

We rebuild the means of production and when we run
out of resources we call the toll-free hotline and ask
for a resumption of the oppressive policies that have
destroyed us for so many centuries

I'm so tired I could sleep on a barbed-wire fence   is not
a sentence you want to say in certain contexts

I'm sorry you think my body reminds you of a South
American vortex whose name you can't pronounce

If the city would explode a bit more politely then we might be able to attract the sorts of entrepreneurs who could finance the futurity of our misery

I mean   what is the first thing you think of when you encounter the spiritual transgression of your body in a tunnel between the absence of time and the hypercirculation of capital?

There's a name for this experience   but I'm not allowed to mention it

The child barking in the tree signals to his neighbors that the tourists are coming with their guns again

The game ends when they recolonize the natives and force them to speak to the wrong god in the wrong language

The new hemisphere appears on the horizon   no one is there to authenticate it

What nation-state controls the sun and the moon? Which hedge fund owns this sea?

We are in the future now but time keeps glitching and the earth keeps quaking backward

You've said this before   *this kidney does not have an owner*

When the war ends they will refine and perfect all that they learned by accident

The most effective ways of reducing the population will become best practices taught at schools throughout the nation

The system requires the authentication of the sacred
body that will never appear

The disappeared body is sanctified and soon the
tourists will pay to see a non-fungible replication of it

The rehumanization of the population repeats itself
first as parody then as encryption

Did you hear the one about the metaphor that was a
metaphor for a metaphor that exists outside thought
and language?

He wanted to kill some time but instead he killed some
villagers

Tough break

In the future   with proper guidance   he'll surely
make better decisions

The Greeks and Romans had a name for this

The foot that despises its slipper

Sustainable Growth #204

In the strange crowds   in the hungry village   on the subway platform
in the history of the lyric

There are corpses everywhere

There are murderous cops everywhere

There are Uber drivers everywhere   corpses everywhere

In 2011   it cost $188 to produce an iPhone

The iPhones sold for $599

The profit margin was 69 percent

No one saw how the workers were chained along the stretch of desert road

They weren't corpses yet   But the bones of their cousins were scattered
in the sand

The profit margin per iPhone decreased 6 percent between 2011 and
2017, yet overall revenues grew 200 percent because of a dramatic rise
in production

There's a dead body in the dumpster behind the dry cleaner's

There's a bouncing coyote in the dumpster behind the television station

There's a time for cooling down and when the cop knocks on my door
and asks me for my number I identify myself and he says why did you
shelter the body and then he sings a song that begins with a conditional
continues in the subjunctive   ends with an imperative   an unanswerable
question   an insult   a beating

The bed is not a place of peace   there are bodies under the bed   there
are children hiding with the bodies under the bed   dead dogs   the

history of our reproduction   the history of the skin they ripped from our arms   of the dead skin that fell from our hands   of the gunk in our eyeballs   of our hair follicles

We can analyze the corpses by talking about the circulation of capital interest on loans   the social relations of labor   the relationship between money and value   the regulation and deregulation of markets the love between user and operating system about which so many romantic comedies are now made

Or   we could talk about murder

It's indecent to ask why one man is so rich when another is so poor

Private property sustains itself while creating dead bodies and inciting the revolution of the proletariat

Unmelodious sentence

The white fathers are disenfranchised

There are corpses in the white fathers' closets

The average retailer makes a 400 percent profit on a dead body

It doesn't cost much to make a dead body in countries without unions or labor regulations

To get back to a 3 percent growth rate   which most economists argue is necessary for sustainable capitalism   we will need to destroy ourselves and the planet and the fathers and the sisters and the earth and the sea and the dolphins and political frameworks of the global south and the overdeveloped north and the underdeveloped east

And if we need to use violence to save the planet from total global destruction at the hands of unregulated capitalism   then here   take this baseball bat and smash some windows please   sang the president of the World Bank to the labor union

The revolution had already been commodified but what had yet to be accomplished was the funding of a legitimate resistance movement to be built up then obliterated by the state and its financiers

My neighbor retired with no pension and now he eats rotten vegetables from the dumpster

He left his house one morning and forgot to wear his shoes   he forgot to wear his socks and forgot to wear his pants   he forgot to wear his shirt and he forgot to wear his coat

I'm sorry   he told his children   when they found him with hypothermia near the river

I will never be human again

Performance of Becoming Human #427:
the earthstatebank theatre

this is the bodega where the bank now stands

this is the hospital where the bank now stands

this is the garden where the bank now stands

the earth and the state and the bank conspire in the earthstatebank
theatre to keep the actors from crying just one more moment

let me finish this tantrum   pleads actor #426.53

let me finish the rage I am feeling so acutely

it brings me so much pleasure to throw a tantrum as the bombs are
falling so gently

you see

I was dying in the niche when the earthstatebank theatre made everyone
look at me

she was dying in the desert   you were dying in the sand   they were
dying in the walls

we just wanted to be alone   but the earthstatebank theatre forced us to
live in its communal hole

and as we performed for the earthstatebank theatre a city broke open in
the hole

the algorithms that destroyed the cities broke open

there was a landscape in the earthstatebank theatre

and in the landscape there were obliterated factories   thousands of
borders   men who beat children as a profession   citizens who beat
noncitizens as a profession

come work for us   beams a billboard in the lobby of the earthstatebank
theatre

beat all the illegal bodies you want and throw in a few legal ones too

an unarmed motorist in the earthstatebank theatre is a body waiting to
be obliterated beyond repair

bienvenida a la tierra sanctificada   bienvenida a la ciudad de tu origen
bienvenida al momento más tranquilo de tu vida

did you hear the one   says actor #9843.231A   about the *Amusement
Park of the Americas* division of the earthstatebank theatre

it's fun   says actor #9843.231A

you can be the kidnapper or you can be the kidnapped

you can even be the verb "to kidnap"

in the earthstatebank theatre you get to be the desert or you get to be the
bodies that cross it

you get to be the border patrol or you can simply be the verb "to patrol"

you get to be the bodies dropping and moving dropping and moving
or you can be the earth or you can simply be the verbs "to drop"
"to move"   "to run"   "to crawl"   "to hide"

you can never be the bank

but you can be interest   assets or dividends   you can even be future
projections on expected growth

let me say a few words about the history of the earthstatebank theatre

once upon a time there were cages massacres burning lakes burning walls
burning love burning nights

words carved into bodies

bodies carved into mountains   bodies carved into skyscrapers
tree trunks   factories

(just breathe)   were the words carved into the flesh

(just breathe)   were the words carved into the mouths

(just breathe)   were the words carved into the silences

my poem makes so much so sense   says earthstatebank poet #XB842.1
every time I recite it I get a message on my cell phone

someone will die because of your breath

or

*go back to the mouth man. . . . don't you see all the poems are in the gag. . . .
the gag in the mouths of prisoners numbers 1–499*

lips check blood check sweat check drool check drivel check baba check
check check check check check check check

the gag has been in so many mouths   the poem has been in so many
mouths

the gag and the poem are the same

repeat

the gag and the poem are the same

I repeat   the gag and the poem are the same

repeat

the gag and the poem are a symbol

I repeat

they are a symbol for a gag and a poem

back in the quote-un-quote "real world"

the Little League team smokes meth in the dugout while the firing squad
stands in front of the precinct shooting at the bodies who vote

had a dream   says actor #4912.4   that the earthstatebank theatre was
no more than a series of numbers that people from my childhood kept
shouting at me

first-grade Kevin shouted 89   Jonas from basketball shouted 42

Eli the neighbor shouted 151314151523156327 and we all understood that
each number was a blank space in the universe occupied by an illegal
face we would say goodbye to when the bank sprouted up where the
earth used to be

ain't nothing to do but drink and accumulate debt in the earthstatebank
theatre   says actor #4912.4   because we cannot separate who we are
from what we owe

let's call the lenders "God's breath"   say the administrators at the
earthstatebank theatre

there's a small bit of humanity in my vacuum cleaner   says actor
#4214.342   during his final soliloquy

let's prepare the audience   she says   for the epiphany at the end of
this poem

close your eyes
breathe
just breathe and repeat

its not love and it's not evil
it's just a small bit of humanity
trapped in your vacuum cleaner
the better to sweep your floors with   my dear
the better to suck up
decades of bone and skin

Lake Michigan, Scene #2123

the first blow comes

then the blank feeling dips

and rises

you and the blank feeling go up

it breathes in and out

goes down and up and down and up

and you breathe in the different scenes

your blank body in the blankest blank of blankness

the train stops and the shadow you have become steps inside

you are underground with the other shadows and when you come into
the night

you see how the lake forms over the city

you see it when you step out of the train

the inverted city

the desiccated lake above the buildings

there is no water anymore

the lake spews its blankness out of your mouth

the darkness in the sky disappears

your ghostbody walks across the frozen city to find you

it wants to know if the day is beginning or ending

you try to answer the question

but your words have no translation

they come out of your mouth in murmurs

in heavy spits   in tongue trips and topples

there are no more images to look at

the sky is in the wrong place

but the breath is here

and your ghostbody is here

and the griefshame is here

and the police are here

and the zone of discounted bodies is here

the lens is here the cage is here the birds the plains the horizon

the water in Chicago disappears again

the darkness of the night sky disappears again

you wrap a thread around your body

to keep your insides from escaping

and when you become ancient again

you sense that   the thing that goes up and goes down

is a barrier that runs through you

a border or a fence or a virus

that can only contain so many absent bodies

beloved is the skin they calculate

beloved is the absence of time

THE MURMURING GRIEF
OF THE AMERICAS

The Murmuring Grief of the Americas

They take the children underground. They tie their hands behind their backs. They put the children in a cage. They tell the children: we have a vision for the future. We will blow up the river. You will blow up the river. Because it's too expensive to maintain it. Together we will blow up the river and we will fill it with pharmaceuticals. There are mufflers and tires floating in the river. There are plastic toys from Asia in the river. There are cell phones in the river. SIM cards and lithium batteries in the river. Cadmium in the river. Cobalt oxide and carbon graphite in the river. There are desperate laborers trying to cross the river. How much should we pay them? ask the authoritative bodies. Market rate? They will love us like we are their parents, say the authoritative bodies. They will protect the pharmaceuticals. They will protect the lithium. They will protect the cobalt. They will protect the carbon and the graphite. They will love the metals and minerals, the enzymes and acids, as if they were their most cherished friends and family.

The Murmuring Grief of the Americas

One morning a man looks at a _____ child he is about to shoot. He sees a structure he cannot build into his life. He sees a language he cannot build into his life. He sees an eye falling out of a face. He sees the cancer of the past reasserting itself into an organism of the present. The organism weeps. The sky weeps. The grass weeps. And the man cannot build this weeping into his life. So he puts the _____ child in a hole with the mourners. But he doesn't like the language in which the mourners grieve. So he teaches them how to grieve in the right language. He teaches them how to weep in the right language. When they lose their eyes he wants to hold their vision in his body. When they lose their mouths he wants to hold their teeth in his body. He wants to own their pain. He wants to own the murmurs they make by sliding their tongues against the roofs of their mouths. He wants to own the murmurs they make by pursing their lips together and opening and closing them slowly. He wants to own their sibilance, their snorts, their silence.

The Murmuring Grief of the Americas

We ask the murmurers what they want to do with
themselves now that they don't get to live anymore.
They say they want to love all the things they could not
love when they were alive. They ask us to carve their
names into the hills and they give us more love than
we have ever known. They hold us and say: You do not
have to survive, you do not have to keep moaning, you
do not have to keep living. What they mean is: in death
we will finally learn about the promise and dignity of
life. We do not recognize the meaning of these words
and we cannot understand why we hear them at this
particular time. The only thing we want to know is:
how can we not become the history of the dead road,
the history of the dead water, the history of the dead
dirt, the history of our children whose bodies will
never grow.

The hole they dig in the street is deep enough to fill with the bodies the police murder. They do not need to cram the bodies into the hole. The bodies fit comfortably into the earth. They do not need to squeeze the bodies into the hole. They do not need to burn the bodies. They treat the bodies better in death than they do in life. There is no decomposition. There is only composition. The dead bodies accumulate as if they are the currency that has long been promised by the agents of power and money.

The Murmuring Grief of the Americas

They ask us what we are doing at Target and we tell them we need to buy sheets. We cannot pronounce our words correctly and they say you need to buy shits you need to buy shits. And they arrest us and laugh at us and tell the manager of the store that we look like shit and smell like shit and ha ha ha isn't it funny that we need to buy shit and in our dreams we throw up on them. Our vomit is purple like the dirty milk they jam into our bodies. They have snakes in their hair and they say: We are fighting to protect the revolution of the endangered white man. They suck us in and suck us out and show us pictures of their motorboats destroyed in last year's hurricane. Just debris now, they say. And they tell us the rain is our fault. They say we are like the evil wind that blows through the Carolinas. They say: You are lucky to have your lives. They say: We hate you because you are what we are not. May your bodies fill with disease.

The Murmuring Grief of the Americas

First come the winds. They are so light we can barely
feel them. The moist air hangs above the hills and when
the rain falls there is no thunder to move it. There is
only a huge storm and a light wind and the cloud mass
forms a smaller cloud mass and soon there are cloud
masses waiting to take their revenge. The authoritative
bodies want to change the weather but their science is
all wrong. The air pressure is too low and the rain falls
and falls and so do the rocks, so do the trees, so do the
hills and houses. When the town is obliterated by the
flood, the murderers pay $150 million to rebuild it. But
they cannot bring back the bodies who lie dead in the
debris. Blessed are the hills that survive. Blessed are
the hills that die.

ACKNOWLEDGMENTS

With thanks to the editors of the following journals who published earlier versions of some of these poems: AGNI; *Big Other; Black Warrior Review; Dialogist; Fence; Georgia Review; Jubilat; Laurel Review; Midst; The Nation; A Perfect Vacuum; Smartish Pace; Spoon River; Tyger Quarterly*

Some sources:

The Complete Poems of César Vallejo, translated by Valentino Gianuzzi and Michael Smith

The Hour of the Star by Clarice Lispector, translated by Benjamin Moser

Architecture of Dispersed Life: Selected Poetry of Pablo de Rokha, translated by Urayoán Noel

Lo Terciario/The Tertiary by Roque Raquel Salas Rivera

The Tennis Court Oath by John Ashbery

The Complete Emily Dickinson

With gratitude to: Kristin Dykstra, Urayoán Noel, Roque Raquel Salas Rivera, Fred Schmalz, Susy Bielak, Stacy Hardy, Kaushik Sunder Rajan, Susan Briante, Sawako Nakayasu, Fady Joudah, Justin Petropoulos, Paula Ilabaca Nuñez, Cecilia Vicuña, Raúl Zurita, Rosa Alcalá, Harris Feinsod, Emily Licht, Michael Dowdy, Joe and Wendy Pan, Adam Novy, Amina Cain, Amarnath Ravva, Bill Marsh, Jose-Luis Moctezuma, Edgar Garcia, Tova Benjamin, Galo Ghigliotto, Carlos Soto Román, Thomas Rothe, Alec Schumacher, Steve Halle, Olivia Lott, David Rojas, Sarah Dodson, Valerie Mejer, Don Mee Choi, Vincent Toro, Achy Obejas, Martin Espada, Brenda Cardenas, Roberto Harrison, and too many others to name.

And so many thanks to Erika Stevens, Abbie Phelps, Laura Graveline, Mark Haber, Quynh Van, and everyone at Coffee House Press.

All love to Rachel Galvin and Lorenzo and Felix Borzutzky—for every single moment of it!

Coffee House Press began as a small letterpress operation in 1972 and has grown into an internationally renowned nonprofit publisher of literary fiction, essay, poetry, and other work that doesn't fit neatly into genre categories.

Coffee House is both a publisher and an arts organization. Through our *Books in Action* program and publications, we've become interdisciplinary collaborators and incubators for new work and audience experiences. Our vision for the future is one where a publisher is a catalyst and connector.

LITERATURE
is not the same thing as
PUBLISHING

Funder Acknowledgments

Coffee House Press is an internationally renowned independent book publisher and arts nonprofit based in Minneapolis, MN; through its literary publications and *Books in Action* program, Coffee House acts as a catalyst and connector—between authors and readers, ideas and resources, creativity and community, inspiration and action.

Coffee House Press books are made possible through the generous support of grants and donations from corporations, state and federal grant programs, family foundations, and the many individuals who believe in the transformational power of literature. This activity is made possible by the voters of Minnesota through a Minnesota State Arts Board Operating Support grant, thanks to the legislative appropriation from the Arts and Cultural Heritage Fund. Coffee House also receives major operating support from the Amazon Literary Partnership, Jerome Foundation, Literary Arts Emergency Fund, McKnight Foundation, and the National Endowment for the Arts (NEA). To find out more about how NEA grants impact individuals and communities, visit www.arts.gov.

Coffee House Press receives additional support from Bookmobile; the Buckley Charitable Fund; Dorsey & Whitney LLP; the Gaea Foundation; the Schwab Charitable Fund; and the U.S. Bank Foundation.

The Publisher's Circle of Coffee House Press

Publisher's Circle members make significant contributions to Coffee House Press's annual giving campaign. Understanding that a strong financial base is necessary for the press to meet the challenges and opportunities that arise each year, this group plays a crucial part in the success of Coffee House's mission.

Recent Publisher's Circle members include many anonymous donors, Patricia A. Beithon, Theodore Cornwell, Jane Dalrymple-Hollo, Mary Ebert & Paul Stembler, Randy Hartten & Ron Lotz, Amy L. Hubbard & Geoffrey J. Kehoe Fund of the St. Paul & Minnesota Foundation, Hyde Family Charitable Fund, Cinda Kornblum, Gillian McCain, Mary & Malcolm McDermid, Vance Opperman, Mr. Pancks' Fund in memory of Graham Kimpton, Robin Preble, Steve Smith, and Paul Thissen.

For more information about the Publisher's Circle and other ways to support Coffee House Press books, authors, and activities, please visit www.coffeehousepress.org/pages/donate or contact us at info@coffeehousepress.org.

DANIEL BORZUTZKY is a poet and translator in Chicago. His books include *Written After a Massacre in the Year 2018; The Performance of Becoming Human,* which received the 2016 National Book Award; and *Lake Michigan,* a finalist for the Griffin International Poetry Prize. His most recent translation is Paula Ilabaca Núñez's *The Loose Pearl,* winner of the 2023 PEN Award for Poetry in Translation. His translation of Galo Ghigliotto's *Valdivia* received ALTA's 2017 National Translation Award, and he has also translated collections by Cecilia Vicuña, Raúl Zurita, and Jaime Luis Huenún. He teaches English and Latin American and Latino studies at the University of Illinois Chicago.

The Murmuring Grief of the Americas was designed by
Bookmobile Design & Digital Publisher Services.
Text is set in Ten Oldstyle.